Joan and the Moon

by Abbie Rushton
illustrated by Charlotte Cotterill

OXFORD
UNIVERSITY PRESS

This is Joan.

Joan cannot nap.

She looks at the moon.
What a sight!

Joan sighs.
The moon is so far.

Joan forms a plan.

Joan gets in her boat.
She sets off from the port.

Joan sails into the night.
She will sail to the moon!

It is a long trip.
I said it was far!

It is so dark.
It might rain soon.

The wind picks up.
The boat lurches.

Joan has wet fur.

Joan sails back to the port.
Then she runs into the woods.

Joan curls up next to a pool.

Then Joan looks in the pool.
She sees a yellow light.
The moon!

Joan can have the moon!

Encourage students to use the pictures to retell the story.